UP CLOSE WITH

BUGS

Alexandra Siy and Dennis Kunkel

Holiday House / New York

TO THE WORLD'S MOST-WANTED TEACHERS AND EDUCATORS, especially Deb Monteith, Ellen Crane, Barb Riegel, Matthew Roberts, and Nancy Cowdin; Shanna Mall (and her crew at the Winterberry Charter School in Anchorage); Kerry Ruef and David Melody of the Private Eye Project in Seattle; Amy Watanabe, retired high school teacher at Windward School District, Oahu, Hawaii; Dr. Lara Lee, Iolani High School, Oahu, Hawaii; Joseph Pacific, St. Andrew's Priory, Oahu, Hawaii; and Mrs. Marilyn Fox and Dr. Betsy Kabrick, Shining Mountain Waldorf School in Boulder, Colorado.

ACKNOWLEDGMENTS

Dennis Kunkel, Alexandra Siy, and the Publisher would like to acknowledge:

Mark C. Mescher, assistant professor at the Center for Chemical Ecology in the Department of Entomology at Pennsylvania State University, for checking this manuscript for accuracy.

Scott Campbell, laboratory director at the Arthropod-Borne Disease Laboratory, Suffolk County Department of Health Services, for providing specimens of carrion beetles, phoretic mites, and rove beetles.

David Sikes, assistant professor in the Department of Entomology at the University of Alaska Museum, for identification of the carrion beetles.

Michael Ivie, associate professor and curator in the Department of Entomology at Montana State University, for the identification of the carrion beetles.

Heather Proctor, professor in the Department of Biological Sciences at the University of Alberta, for identification of the phoretic mites.

David Walker, acarologist and taxonomic adviser in the Alberta Biodiversity Monitoring Institute at the Royal Alberta Museum, for identification of the phoretic mites.

Terry Lynch, naturalist, photographer, and creator of Firefly FAQs at www.firefly.byteland.org, for providing specimens of fireflies.

James Lloyd, retired professor in the Department of Entomology and Nematology at the University of Florida, for providing specimens of fireflies.

Editors Mary Cash and Sylvie Frank, and Art Director Claire Counihan for their vision and hard work on this book.

CONTENTS

WANTED

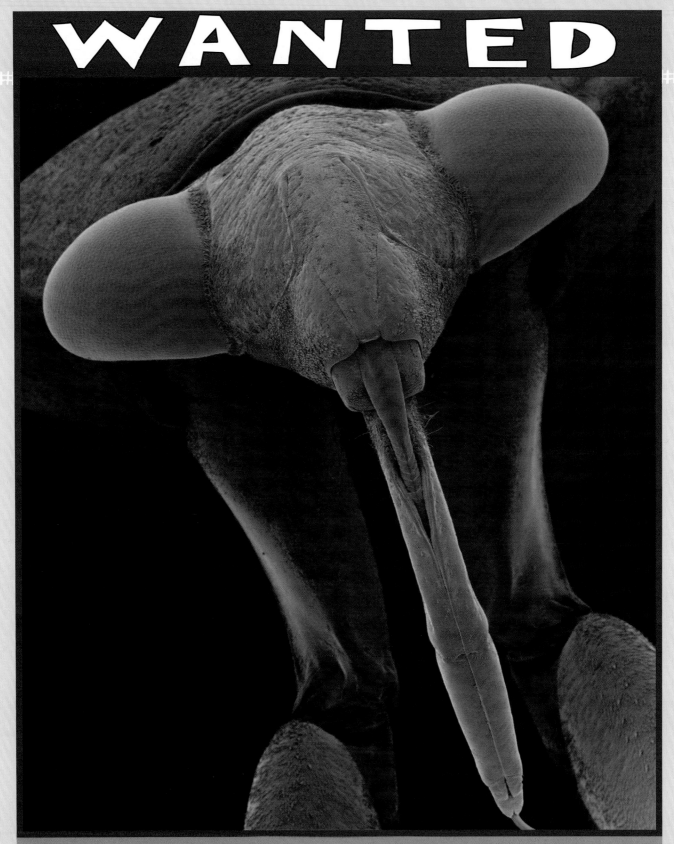

This giant water bug is shown 28 times (x28) larger than its actual size. The photographs in this book are photomicrographs taken through a scanning electron microscope (SEM). The original image is black and white. The micrograph is colored to highlight structures.

Bugs bite. Some drink blood. Bugs rob. They steal food from gardens and fields. Bugs kill—mostly each other, but also plants, animals, even people sometimes. Bugs destroy. They eat houses, clothes, and furniture. Bugs bug. (Is bugging a crime?)

Accused criminals get a fair trial. They are assumed innocent until proven guilty. Bugs deserve justice, too. Study their mug shots, read their rap sheets. Join the FBI—become a *Fellow Bug Investigator*. This requires grit, guts, and gall. Fellow Bug Investigators must be prepared to enter foreign territory and do the dirty work. Their motto: *First Become Insect*. Look into a bug's eyes, then try to imagine the world through them. Consider all the evidence. Don't throw the book at a bug until you're convinced beyond a reasonable doubt: good, bad, or bugly. The jury is still out.

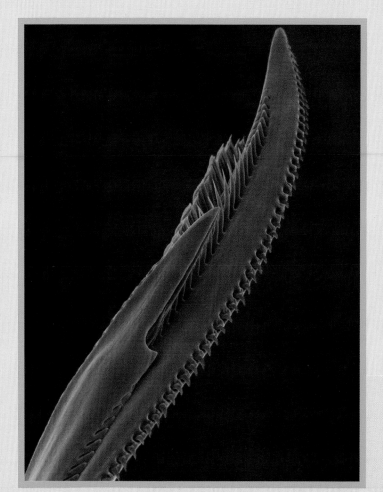

How can you tell the difference between a good bug and a bad one? After all, bad guys often pretend to be nice when they're really liars, thieves, kidnappers, or killers. Do insects play sneaky tricks, too? Pay attention to a bug's "smile"—nasty or nice, it's a clue to its identity.

The proboscis of a giant water bug is a mouthlike organ. It is used for feeding on other insects as well as on tadpoles, salamanders, small fish, and snails. True bugs have sucking, beak-shaped mouths. (x345)

Speaking strictly scientifically, only some insects are truly bugs. True bugs belong to the insect order called Hemiptera, which means "half-wings." The bottom parts of their front wings are thick; the tips are tissue-paper-thin. True bugs have beak-shaped mouths that curve like a backward letter C. They eat by stabbing their beaks into plants, fruit, and animals, including people. Then they suck sap, fruit juice, or blood (now, that's bad).

All insects belong to a huge group of related animals called arthropods (which means "jointed legs"). Insects make up the group, or *class*, called Insecta, which is further divided into thirty-two groups called *orders*. Although they are related, members of different orders have bodies that look very different (compare a butterfly to an ant).

The house fly belongs to the order Diptera, which means "two wings." Flies have two wings, while insects in most other orders have four (two pairs). (x27)

Picture the orders as thirty-two big metal FBI file cabinets. Inside each drawer are bulging files labeled with *family* names. Members of a family are more closely related and are divided again into color-coded folders—each color representing a different *genus*. What's inside one of these colorful folders? Rap sheets, of course! One rap sheet for every *species*. Members of a species are so closely related that they can mate and have young. They are wanted, dead and alive.

This view of the house fly shows its three-part body plan: head, with its large compound eyes; thorax, where the wings and legs attach; and abdomen, which contains internal organs such as the heart. The scientific name of the house fly is *Musca domestica*. (x35)

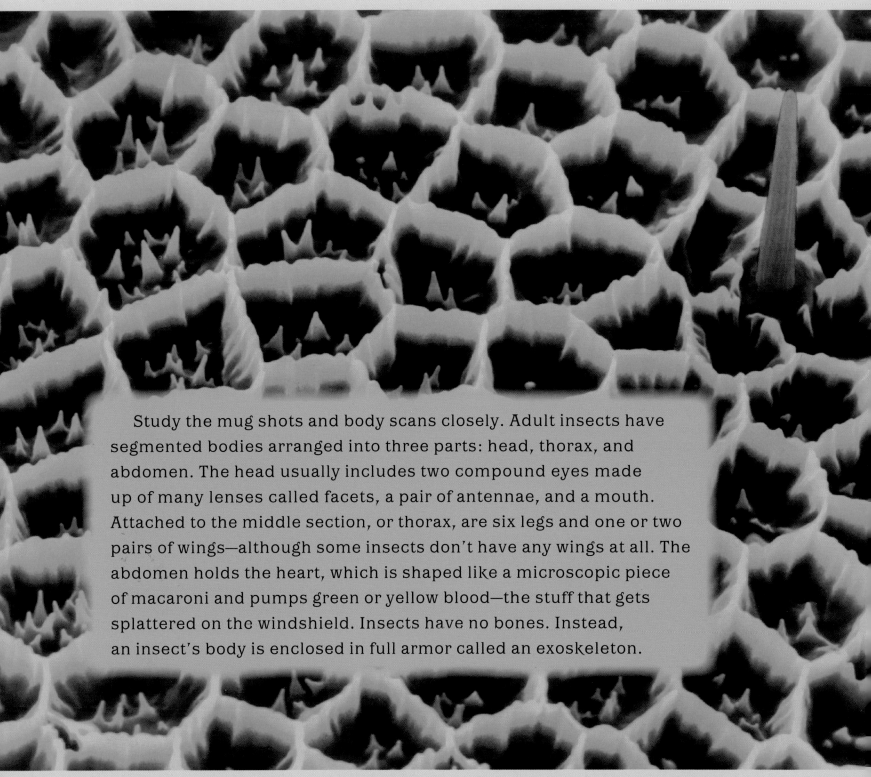

Study the mug shots and body scans closely. Adult insects have segmented bodies arranged into three parts: head, thorax, and abdomen. The head usually includes two compound eyes made up of many lenses called facets, a pair of antennae, and a mouth. Attached to the middle section, or thorax, are six legs and one or two pairs of wings—although some insects don't have any wings at all. The abdomen holds the heart, which is shaped like a microscopic piece of macaroni and pumps green or yellow blood—the stuff that gets splattered on the windshield. Insects have no bones. Instead, an insect's body is enclosed in full armor called an exoskeleton.

The exoskeleton of a grasshopper is made of a tough, waterproof material called chitin. Its structure, which looks like a chain-link fence, makes it strong. Grasshoppers belong to the order Orthoptera, which means "straight wings." (x3,260)

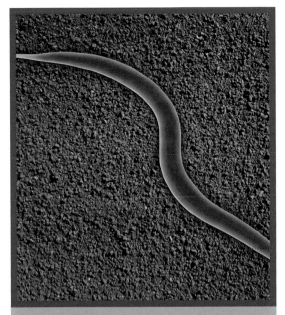

Tiny nematode worms are not insects! They live in the soil, where they help decompose rotting plant material. (x310)

Being an FBI agent can be tough—successfully spying on and identifying suspects is demanding. There are more species of insects than any other kind of animal. Entomologists, scientists who study insects, have discovered more than 900,000 insect species. (That's a lot of rap sheets.) Researchers think there could be at least 5 million. Yet insects are not the most common animals on Earth. When counting individuals, four out of five animals on the planet are nematode worms.

Altogether, how many species of plants, animals, and microscopic bacteria and viruses inhabit Earth? About 1.5 million are named, but scientists estimate there could be anywhere between 10 million and 100 million different species. That's a whole lot of life left to track down!

Now, think of this: human beings are one species with more than 7 billion (7,000,000,000) living members. Compare that to the 1 quintillion (1,000,000,000,000,000,000) individual insects populating the planet at any moment. That's almost 150 million insects for every man, woman, and child!

As an FBI agent, remember: just like people, the vast majority of insects are helpful—only a few types are destructive, dangerous, or downright deadly. In both cases, it's important to know who is who.

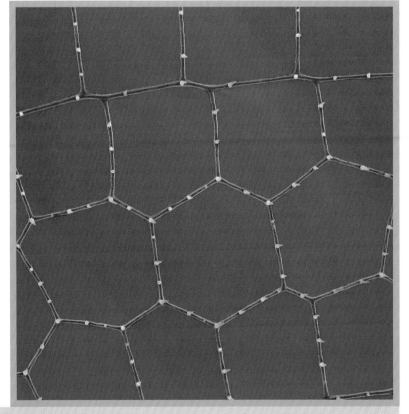

This is part of a dragonfly wing. A network of veins creates interlocking pieces that make the wing strong and beautiful, like panes in a stained glass window. Dragonflies belong to the order Odonata, which means "tooth mouth." They have two pairs of long wings that help them fly fast as they hunt mosquitoes and other insects. (x35)

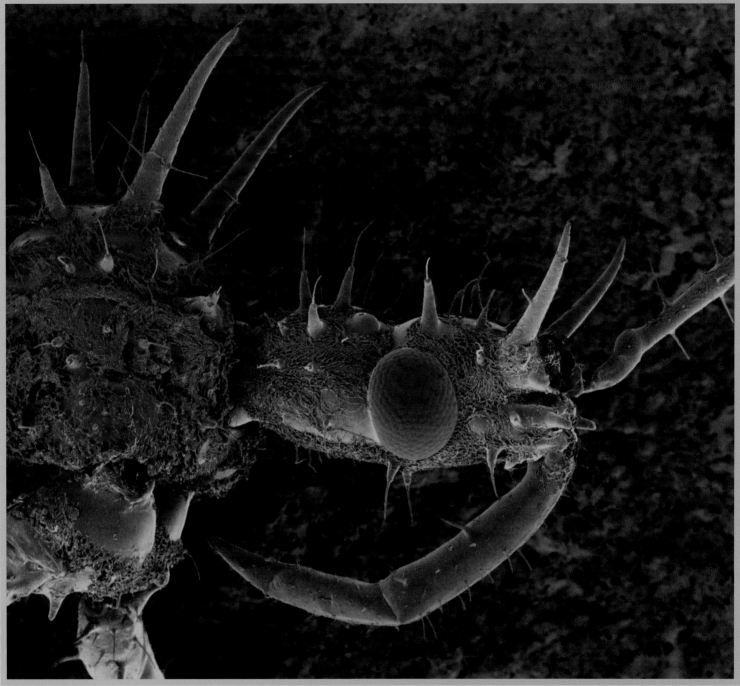

True bugs, such as this assassin bug, have a long, slender, segmented beak. Most species of assassin bugs hunt other insects. An assassin pins down its prey with its front legs and stabs it with its beak. Saliva is injected into the victim, dissolving the insides into food for the assassin to drink. Count the segments on its beak: one, two, three (some true bug beaks have four). (x51)

Start an investigation with obvious suspects such as parasites and pests. Insect parasites live on or inside a host plant or animal. Some are true bugs, many are pests, and most pests are wanted dead.

Assassin bugs look more frightening, but the comparatively cute bedbug is among the "most wanted" of all. During the day it hides and waits on the mattress or in a crack in the wall. Then, in the middle of the night, it sneaks out and crawls onto its sleeping victim. It stabs its beak through its host's skin and sucks blood. It prefers people to pets (people don't have fur) but will take what it can get. Its eggs hitchhike across the globe on people's clothes and luggage. Some bedbug species live outdoors, attacking birds and bats.

It could be worse. Bedbugs aren't the worst villains. Some blood-sucking insects carry diseases. Mosquitoes are at the top of the most-wanted list. They are the deadliest animals on Earth. About twenty mosquito species carry malaria, a disease that kills at least 1 million people every year.

A bedbug is a flat, oval-shaped, reddish brown bug about the same size across as a pencil eraser. (x22)

People and pets aren't a bug's only victims. Lace bugs pierce the leaves of bushes and trees such as alder, ash, avocado, azalea, birch, and willow, then drink the sugary sap inside.

Don't panic. People often think poisonous, pest-killing chemicals called pesticides are the only protection. Lace bugs and many other pests have natural enemies. Assassin bugs, ladybird beetles, and jumping spiders gobble up lace bugs.

The azalea lace bug has delicate, lacy wings. The female lays her eggs inside a leaf so that newly hatched bugs can feed immediately. (x14)

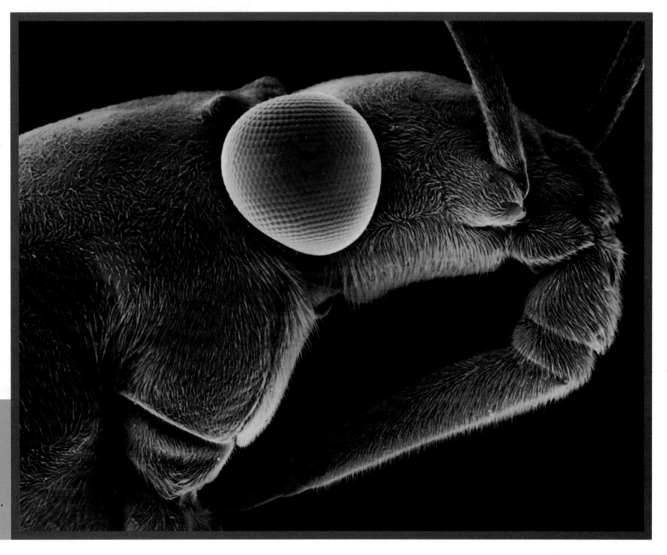

Water striders glide on water by moving one pair of legs in a manner similar to rowboat oars. (x57)

Most true bugs are harmless to humans. Inspect the adorable water strider, which walks on water and grabs insects that tumble from the shore. There are good guys galore. Get outside and check them out.

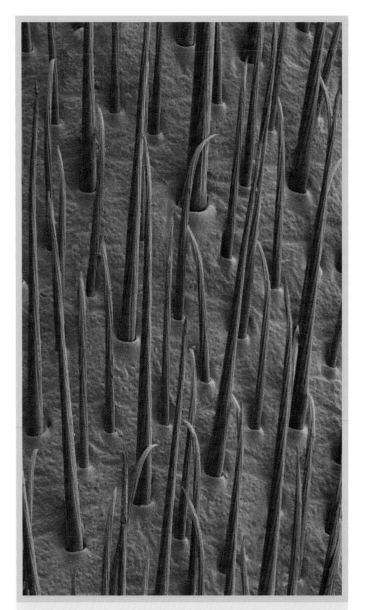

The water strider has a thick layer of fine hairs, called microsetae, on its legs. The water strider has six legs: two shortened forelegs catch prey, two middle legs lay flat on the water and row the insect along, and two hind legs support and steer the insect. (x665)

Zooming in on the strider's leg shows the physical structure and arrangement of the microsetae. Each tiny hair is notched with grooves (measured in nanometers, or billionths of a meter). Air gets trapped in the grooves, forming an air cushion that allows the insect to float. (x2,100)

WANTED

The ladybird beetle has large, shiny front wings (called elytra) that cover the longer hind wings, which are folded when the insect is resting. During flight, the front wings are raised, allowing the thin and flexible hind wings to move. (x48)

Some mugs look harmless. Many insects are. A ladybug isn't actually a bug but a beetle. Ladybugs, properly called ladybird beetles, are pretty and popular—even the "guys." (There are male and female ladybugs despite their name.) People admire them for their bright red, yellow, or orange colors and striking black markings. Also appreciated are their appetites. Many ladybug species dine on plant-eating pests, such as aphids and mites.

Beetles are the most common kind of insect, forming the largest order, Coleoptera, which means "sheath wing." Beetles have thick, hard front wings (elytra) that encase the thin hind wings that many species use for flying—although some species do not fly at all. However, all have mouths that chomp and chew.

The mug shots of the beetles can be quite different from one another. So can their lifestyles. Beetles can be smaller than a sugar crystal—the feather-winged beetle is a fraction of a millimeter long—or as enormous as a king-size candy bar—the tropical Goliath beetle is 200 millimeters (8 inches) long and up to 75 millimeters (3 inches) wide.

The pepper weevil's mouth is on the tip of its snout. It eats by pushing its mouth into a vegetable, where it chews away at the nutritious insides. A dark speck on a pepper is a clue that a weevil was there. Like most beetles it has two sets of wings. Shown here is a hind wing slipping out of the crack between the leathery front wings (elytra). (x30)

15

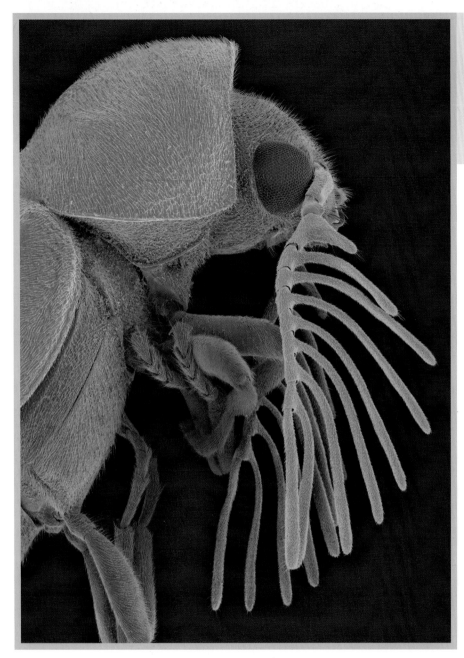

The adult male deathwatch beetle doesn't eat anything. He attracts a female by tapping his jaws on the wooden wall of his tunnel. His shaggy antennae (green) detect a female's chemical signals. After mating, the female lays her eggs in cracks in wood. The eggs hatch into wood-eating larvae that make openings for decomposing fungi and bacteria to enter. (x43)

The tortoise beetle has a brilliant golden or silver circular body shaped like (surprise) a tiny tortoise shell, while the long, skinny pinhole borer's shape allows it to tunnel deep into trees. The body of the flat bark beetle fits under bark, where it eats tiny insects. The shining flower beetle is glossy black and nearly spherical—like a marble. Some beetles have long snouts (the snout weevils, naturally) or horns on their heads (rhinoceros beetles). Others have big, shaggy antennae (deathwatch beetles) or mammoth mouths (stag beetles). Beetles can be dazzlingly decorated like some of the leaf beetles or drab and dull like the mold-eating minute brown scavenger beetle.

Can a common criminal be flashy? The lightning bug, also known as the firefly, is neither a true bug nor a fly, but a beetle (of course). There are about 2,000 species of fireflies, and each one puts on its own signature light show. Fireflies communicate in flashes. The males flicker as they fly, while down in the grass the females watch. When a female sees the pattern of blinks from a male of her species, she flashes back. All night long, a female flashes back and forth with many males. At the end of the night she chooses only one to be her mate. Then she lays her eggs in the grass. The glowing larvae live on the ground, surviving on worms, slugs, and snails.

A picture of bugliness, this common firefly shows off her lovely orange and yellow painted "toenails." Her leg tarsus, pulvillar pad, and claw are shown below at increasing magnifications. (x14)

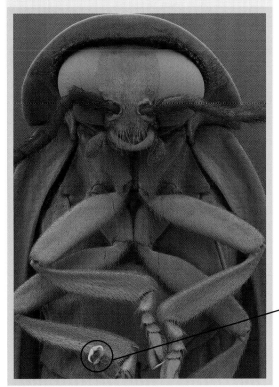

The claw and pulvillar pad help the common firefly cling and stick to a blade of grass. Tenent setae on the pulvillar pad secrete a sticky goo. (x120)

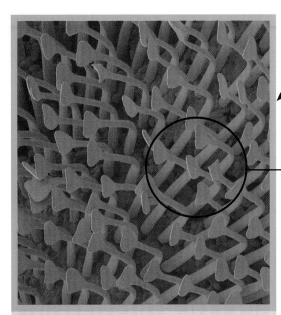

Here the tenent setae are magnified to show their spatula-shaped structure. (x795)

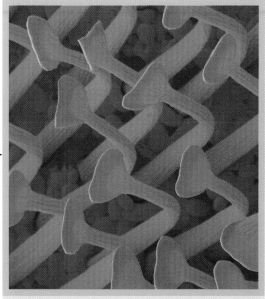

Ultraclose view of the firefly tenent setae. (x1,850)

This is a female predator firefly called *Photuris*. Note the large jaws called mandibles (bright orange) that catch, snip, and kill. *Photuris* species are sometimes referred to as "femme fatale fireflies." (x30)

Adult fireflies of most species do not eat—they're too busy flitting and flirting. But sometimes the sexiest flashes attract the wrong sort of character. *Photuris* is a predator firefly that attacks, kills, and devours other fireflies. It tricks males of other species by pretending to be a friendly female, then snatches them when they get too close. *Photuris* also attacks like a stealth enemy fighter plane, swooping down from the night sky to destroy its unsuspecting victims. Perhaps *Photuris* is more double agent than common criminal....

Fascinating, flashy, or felonious, all beetle mugs have one thing in common: they possess mouths that chew side to side (humans chew up and down). In some species only the larval stage eats. Chomping their way through crops, forests, flour, clothing, and even museum specimens, some beetles are considered enemies of the people and are wanted dead.

But what would a world without beetles really be like? Picture a planet piled high with poop and the dead carcasses of plants and animals. Dung beetles roll great big balls of poop—it's their main course. Flesh-eating beetles devour dead animal bodies. After all, animals and plants die from accidents, disease, and old age just like people. Someone needs to clean up the mess. There are beetles in the forest, in the fields, underwater, under rocks, inside logs, in the dirt, in the garbage, tidying up Earth 24-7.

Could insects be getting a bad rap?

This is a carrion beetle and a phorectic mite (shown in orange). After breeding on small carrion (dead animal carcass), male and female carrion beetles dig the ground under the carcass to bury it along with their eggs. When the eggs hatch, the larvae eat the carcass, transform into pupae, and then become adults. Often carrion beetles are covered with tiny phorectic mites, which get carried from carcass to carcass. These mites feed on the eggs of flies and are not in competition with the carrion beetle larvae for food. (x73)

The proboscis of the woodland skipper butterfly is coiled when the insect is at rest. When feeding, the proboscis uncurls and dips into flowers from which it sips nectar. (x125)

4. BUTTERFLIES AND MOTHS: CHANGING IDENTITIES

Evidence indicates that lots of insects are upstanding citizens. Imagine a world without them—it might also be a world without blueberries, almonds, chocolate, or evening primrose oil. Insects are pollinators—they transfer pollen grains from the male part of one flower (the anther) to the female part (the stigma) of another. When a pollen grain comes together with an egg inside a flower, a seed is formed. The fruit, such as a blueberry, grows around the seeds.

Bees of many species pollinate blueberry bushes and almond trees. Cacao trees produce cocoa beans for chocolate and are pollinated by pinhead-size flies called midges. Moths pollinate the sweetly perfumed blossoms of flowers such as jasmine and evening primrose.

Most moths are active at night and feed from flowers that reflect moonlight from pale-colored petals. Their feathery antennae detect a blossom's fragrant scent.

The compound eye of a moth is made of hexagon-shaped lenses (called ommatidia) that see colors, shapes, and movement but do not focus clear, detailed images. (x5,190)

The monarch butterfly has a large compound eye (orange) and long proboscis (olive green). Pollen sticks to its "hairy" head and is carried from flower to flower. (x17)

A butterfly relies more on its sense of vision than on its sense of smell. Its big eyes can see colorful flowers. Its long, flexible mouthpart, called a proboscis, dips into flowers and sips nectar, the ultimate high-energy drink. A butterfly can also taste using sensory receptors on its feet as it grips the edge of the flower petal. The butterfly's hairy head works like a dust mop, picking up pollen. Pollination happens when the pollen-covered "dust mop" brushes against a sticky stigma—picture glitter on glue.

Shown here is a monarch butterfly's leg and claw, which grips flower petals. Taste receptors on its front feet help it find milkweed plants, where the female monarch lays her eggs. (x31)

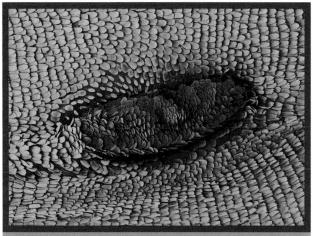

The scent glands (brown) found on a male monarch butterfly's hind wings make a chemical perfume that attracts females. (x18)

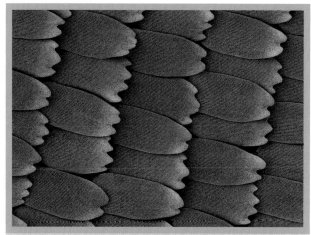

These are monarch butterfly wing scales. The overlapping pattern makes the wings strong and waterproof. (x135)

Moths and butterflies belong to the insect order called Lepidoptera, which means "scale wing." But these gorgeous fliers started out as something else entirely.

Clever suspects can escape capture by changing their identities. Others are masters of disguise. All insects change throughout their lifetimes. To grow, insects must molt by shedding their old armor after growing a new exoskeleton underneath.

Some insects, such as the true bugs, hatch from their eggs looking like miniature, wingless copies of adults.

Most insects, however, hatch as larvae called caterpillars, grubs, maggots, or worms, depending on the species. Looking and behaving quite differently from their adult parents, the very hungry larvae eat, grow, and molt (several times), wiggling all the while. Then, like suspects in hiding, they spin a cocoon or encase themselves in a puparium. When they come out, they are totally transformed. The adult looks nothing like its previous self—a complete metamorphosis has taken place.

This egg was laid by a monarch butterfly on the lower surface of a milkweed leaf. Newly hatched caterpillars feed on milkweed leaves, their sole source of food. Milkweed contains a poison that is harmless to monarchs but makes them taste bad to birds and other monarch predators. (x36)

WANTED

The honeybee has a tongue that is kept tightly folded against its head when the insect is not feeding. A honeybee's compound eyes can see blue and yellow flowers, as well as ultraviolet light, which is invisible to humans. (x38)

5. BEES, ANTS, AND WASPS: PARTNERS IN CRIME

Some insects are armed and considered dangerous. Their stingers are like concealed weapons, instilling fear and inflicting pain. Should these hooligans enter a plea of self-defense, or are there other legitimate explanations for their aggressive behavior?

Bees can "get away with murder" because they are superstars. They pollinate most of our fruit, many of our vegetables, and even crops such as cotton—no bees, no tees. Worldwide there are about 20,000 bee species. Ninety percent live alone, building one-insect nests (think pup tents) on the ground or on the stems of plants. Bees, along with ants and wasps, belong to the order Hymenoptera, which means "membrane wing."

The most famous bee is the honeybee, and it's wanted alive everywhere, even in New York City, where it used to be an outlaw. Illegal beekeepers worked together to educate lawmakers about the tremendous benefits of honeybees. In 2010, beekeeping in NYC was legalized, and hundreds of decriminalized beekeepers danced for joy!

Female bees have a stinger, which is a modified ovipositor (egg-laying organ). Since only the queen lays eggs, a worker's stinger is used for protecting the hive from honey thieves. A worker dies after she stings an intruder because her stinger is ripped from her body as she flies away. (x63)

Pollen (small specks) sticks to the hairs (setae) on a honeybee's head and is carried from flower to flower. The two brown structures are the bee's antennae. (x100)

This is a setae, or hair, from the backside of a honeybee. Many insects have setae, but only bees have branch-shaped setae, which help them collect pollen. Pollen is a high-protein food for larvae and adults. (x1,190)

Honeybees are social insects that live in colonies of up to 50,000 members. Worker bees, which are all female, do everything—from collecting food, building the hive, and making honey to caring for the young. Males mate . . . but only with the queen. The queen can lay 2,000 eggs a day.

The honeybee colony is a superorganism—the entire group works together like a single living thing. The secret of its success is communication. Honeybees don't talk, but they can dance and send messages with scents. A little perfume goes a long way.

Spying into the secret world of a dark hive, we see a forager bee waggling her abdomen as she moves in a circle. Her body is dusted with a flower's tasty scent. Several of her sisters press close. The bees use their antennae to smell and taste the dancer's body and feel the air swirling around her wings. The sisters understand the message. It is a set of detailed directions to a particular flower filled with food. The sisters fly to the flower, then home again, their baskets packed with pollen, their stomachs full of nectar.

Many people are fond of bees (who doesn't like honey and beeswax lip balm?) but aren't so taken with their relatives. Wasps and ants often get a bad rap.

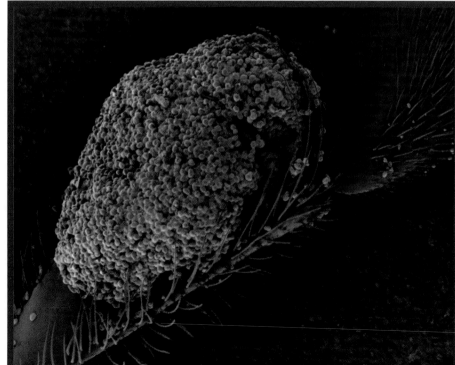

A honeybee's leg has a curve-shaped "basket" for carrying pollen. Setac (blue hairs) help keep the pollen in the basket. (x32)

Ants never act alone—they are true partners in crime. They live in colonies. Working together they are a superorganism. Digging, mixing, tunneling, burrowing, excavating, plowing, turning, hoeing, tilling, and raking, they build nests in soil and rotting wood. Marching, tracking, chasing, hunting, snipping, clipping, gardening, and farming, they are a great big gang of girls on the go. In the process they till the ground, fertilize the soil, and sow seeds. You go, girls!

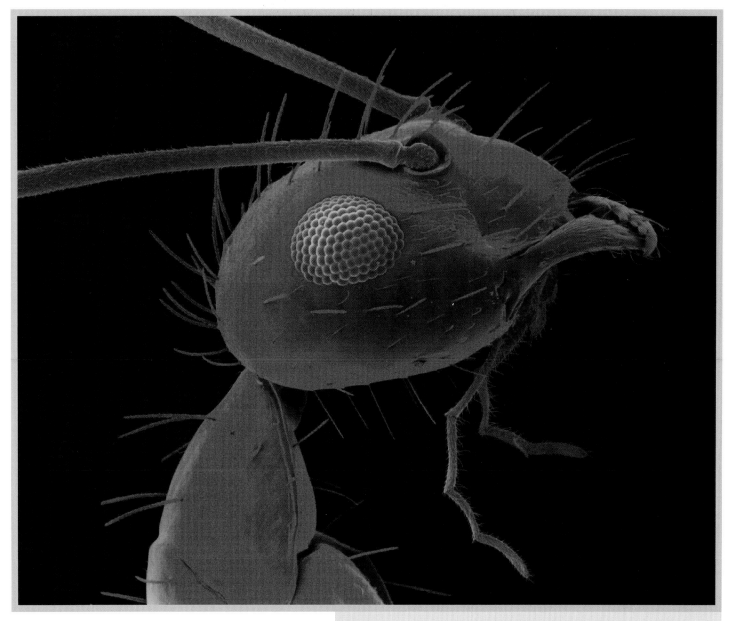

This is a crazy ant, one of 14,000 ant species. Notice her large mandibles (jaws), which collect, carry, and chew food; dig dirt; build nests; and fight. Ants also have tongues that lick and suck. (x110)

Soldiers, diggers, builders, food finders, and babysitters—all are sisters. The brothers, like male bees, mate with the queen and then quickly die. The queen mates once, then lays eggs every day for the rest of her life. In some species the queen can live for twenty years.

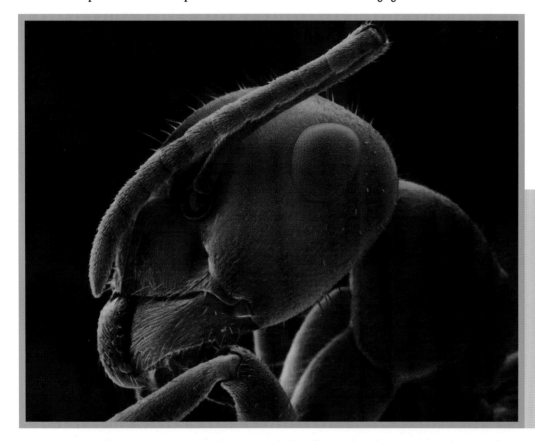

Note the bent ("elbowed") antenna on the head of this red ant. This adaptation helps it follow chemical trails along the ground. Ants also have small compound eyes (red), and some ants lack eyes completely. Ants depend on their senses of smell and taste for communication rather than on vision. (x61)

Ants communicate with chemical concoctions detected by the outer segments of their antennae. Unlike people (whose language depends mostly on sound and sight), ants "talk" in tastes and smells. Ants have many glands that spray at least a dozen different chemical signals, called pheromones. Smelly trails squirted along the ground say *Food this way*. Ants sniff intruders and strangers with their antennae and then spurt them with odor messages that warn *Get out of here before I attack!* They will fight to the death defending their colony, tearing enemies to shreds with powerful jaws. When encountering danger along the trail, they spew chemical clouds that yell *Run away!* And when an ant dies, her sisters lick her corpse to detect the taste that means *I am dead*—then she is carried away to the ant cemetery deep within the nest.

What about wasps? Could they be as astonishing as bees and ants? Like a good detective spying on a suspect, watch a tiny female *Nasonia* wasp stab a blowfly pupa with her ovipositor. Observe as she lays thirty to fifty eggs inside her victim. The eggs hatch within two days, and the larvae feed off of the fly pupa for about nine days before entering their own pupal stage. The adult wasps emerge in three days by chewing a hole through the host's casing.

Wasps employ amazing techniques of ambush, attack, bondage, and torture, resulting in the slow and inevitable death of their prey. These are valuable tactics if you're trying to exterminate crop-destroying insects without the use of toxic chemicals. Wasps may be desperadoes acting alone, but they're perfect partners for a farmer when it comes to getting rid of crop-eating pests.

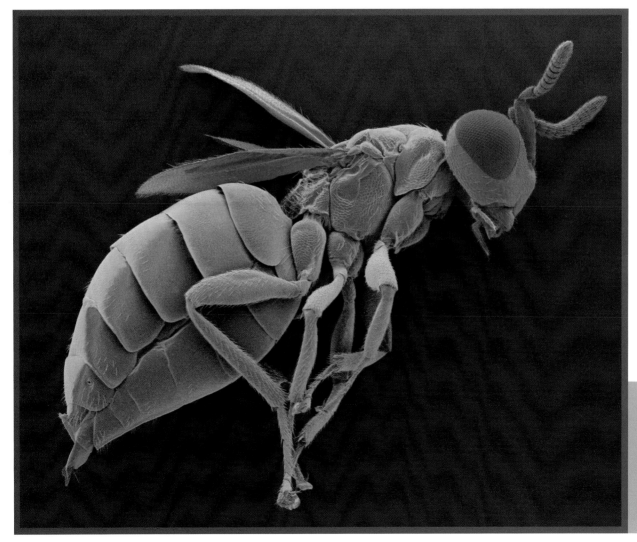

An adult male *Nasonia* wasp is the size of a pinhead. *Nasonia* are used by farmers as a tool for biocontrol (an alternative to chemical control) of pest flies. (x45)

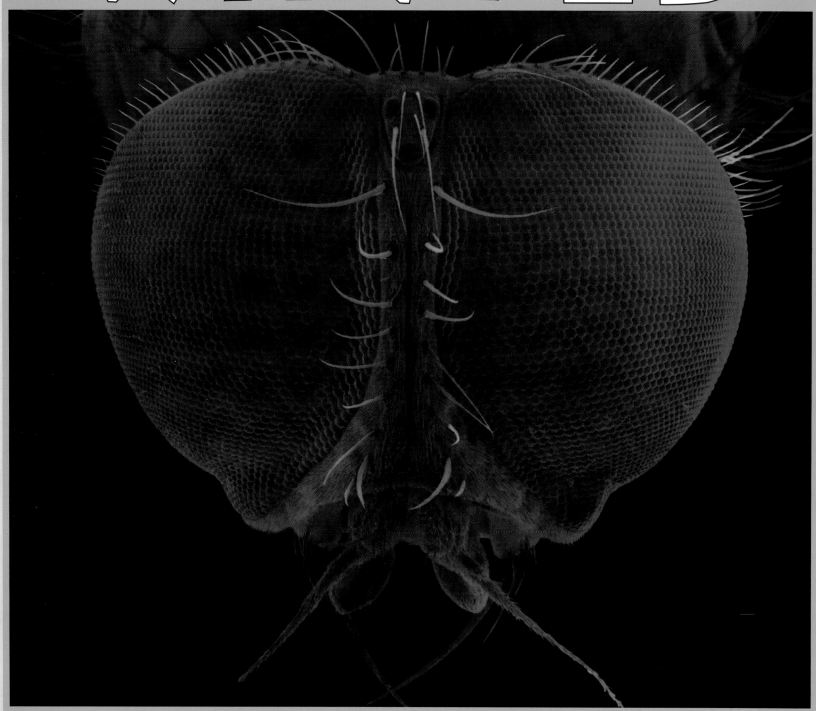

A house fly has large compound eyes composed of hundreds of tiny lenses called ommatidia. (x96)

A fruit fly "swims" through the air using its wings like oars to turn quickly. Its wing joints work like the springs in windup toys. By simply tensing a wing muscle the fly causes the wing to tilt, while air drag whirls the insect up and down and side to side. Scientists hope that their studies of fruit fly aerodynamics will help them design flying robots. (x32)

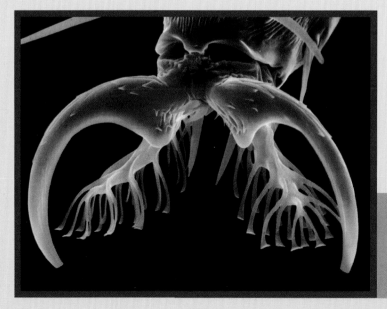

Shown here are a fruit fly leg claw and pulvillar pad ("hairy" foot pad). Flies can walk upside down on ceilings and other smooth surfaces due to the sticky substance released through the tube-shaped tenent setae (purplish pink, feathery structures). (x1,640)

Shouldn't the FBI come down hard on all those dirty, biting, nasty flies that spread germs and transmit disease? (Recall the mosquito: guilty!) They have no alibi! It's obvious they're the ones hovering over the fruit bowl, walking on the kitchen counter, hatching maggots in the trash can, biting the back of your neck. And then they flee the scene. Fugitives too fast for a human hand.

Flies belong to the order Diptera, which means "two wings." Indeed, they have one pair of membranous front flying wings. The second pair of hind wings are tiny knobs that help stabilize the insect as it rapidly changes direction in flight.

A house fly's wings beat 200 times in one second. Its large eyes detect movement as it zigs and zags away from the fly swatter. The sticky setae (microhairs) on its foot pads help it cling safely to the ceiling.

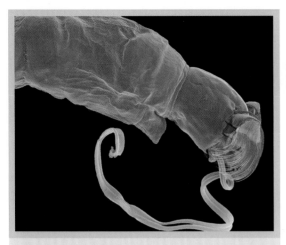

Most insects go through complete metamorphosis similar to that of the black fly. Shown here is a black fly larva. Note the ribbon of silk (blue) coming from the mouth area, which the larva uses to attach to underwater rocks and plants. A head fan (yellow) sweeps food into its mouth. Larvae pass through six instar stages before reaching the pupal stage. (x17)

This black fly pupa is encased in a silken cocoon. The adult black fly emerges from the pupal case through a slit and floats to the surface of the water on a bubble of air. (x11)

The black fly has two compound eyes, short segmented antennae, and skin-piercing mouthparts. Female black flies require a blood meal to nourish their eggs, while males feed mainly on nectar. Adult female black flies lay their eggs in slow-moving waters. (x24)

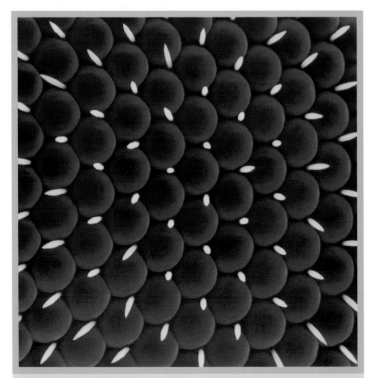

The compound eye of a fruit fly has tiny hairs among the individual ommatidia. (x820)

Female black flies are vicious biters, slicing the skin of birds and mammals (particularly people) and slurping blood to nourish their eggs. Yet these outlaws also fall victim to other animals. Adult and larval forms of flies are food for dragonflies (which are not flies), ants, spiders, birds, bats, tadpoles, frogs, and fish.

Insects have compound eyes made from many tube-shaped facets, or lenses, called ommatidia. A dragonfly with its huge eyes sees in all directions as it hunts fast-flying insects in midair. (Dragonflies are in the order Odonata, which means "tooth mouth.") Some dragonfly species have more than 30,000 facets.

The compound eye of the fruit fly contains 800 facets. The eye of an insect cannot focus to see a clear picture. Instead, it sees many fast-moving identical pictures. Together these pixel-like images create a rapidly changing map of an object's location in space and time—perhaps similar to a movie in fast-forward.

Nocturnal insects, such as moths and fireflies, have a different way of seeing. The inner structure of their compound eyes creates one blurry image rather than many separate pictures. Their eyes are 100 times more sensitive to light than the eyes of insects that are active during the day.

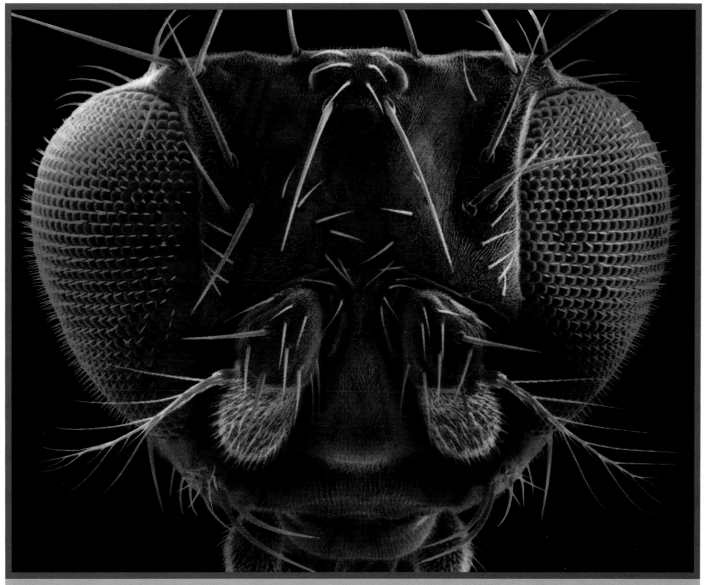

The head of a fruit fly has large compound eyes and short antennae. (x195)

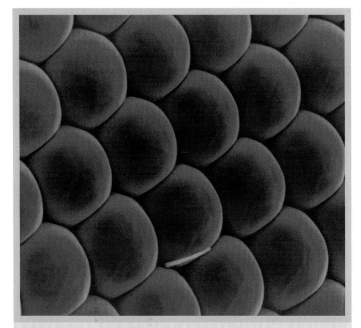

Zooming in on a house fly eye. (x1,500)

The first studies of insect vision were made with a microscope focused so the viewer could actually look through a fly's eye. More than 300 years later, scientists used laser beams to discover the first known case of bifocal vision (two eyes in one) in a living organism. Sunburst diving beetle larvae (called water tigers) have twelve eyes composed of two types of lenses. Some lenses can focus up close and others can look into the distance—a great help for catching fast-swimming prey. Although we have discovered much about *how* an insect sees, can we really know *what* it sees?

Perhaps insects see with their brains, just as we do. Humans form mental pictures based on experience and knowledge. This is perception. We can't recognize what we have never experienced. (That's why we need wanted posters!) Seeing is all about the relationship between a living being and everything else.

We don't know if insects form mental pictures. But we can imagine that all of an insect's senses create the big picture of an alien world we cannot recognize.

This is the wing surface of a bromeliad mosquito. It takes its name from the bromeliad plant whose leaves form a cup that catches water in which the mosquito lays her eggs. Bromeliad mosquitoes are among the smallest mosquitoes and have a maximum life span of about three weeks. (x225)

Scales cover various body parts of most mosquitoes. Shown here are the leg scales from the black salt marsh mosquito. These fierce biters are strong fliers that live and breed in salt marshes. They can transmit parasites, including dog heartworms and disease-causing viruses such as West Nile virus. (x2,040)

Insects make sense of the world in a different time frame and on a different scale from ours. They move rapidly with body parts that are up to a million times smaller than our own. They detect fast motions that to us appear as a blur. They "talk" using chemical smells that are imperceptible to our senses. Their lives are impossibly short—a fly hatches, grows up, mates, and dies all in the course of a month. One month becomes a lifetime. To an insect, does it *feel* like a lifetime—in the human sense of the word?

How can we really know and understand beings that are so different, so foreign, so unusual, so unlike, so unrelated, so strange, so polar opposite, so curious, so bizarre, so outlandish, so utterly odd to us?

7. THE BUGLY: WANTED DEAD AND ALIVE

Good "bug"? Bad "bug"? The jury is in. Judged by human standards, the malaria-carrying *Anopheles* mosquito is guilty beyond any reasonable doubt and wanted dead. Shouldn't it be prosecuted to the fullest extent of the law—capital punishment, extermination, eradication, annihilation, obliteration?

Honeybees, on the other hand, loved and cherished by humans since ancient times, are the perfect picture of bugly goodness. Yet they are threatened by Colony Collapse Disorder (CCD), a catastrophe that wipes out entire colonies. Who should be prosecuted? Bad nutrition (some commercial beekeepers feed their bees high fructose corn syrup), parasitic mites, diseases, stress, and exposure to chemicals are blamed. Maybe we need to listen to the bees—for their good and our own.

Honeybees aren't the only good guys (or should we say gals?) wanted alive. Bumblebees, orchid bees, blue mud wasps, eastern tiger swallowtail butterflies, Cairns birdwing butterflies, blue morpho butterflies, pink-spotted hawkmoths, flower flies, scarab beetles—pollinators all, and that's only the beginning.

Mostly good, sometimes bad, always bugly, insects are wanted—dead and alive.

GUILTY

(x13)

INNOCENT

(x17)

Many people who collected insects when they were children say that the hobby was the beginning of a lifelong love for nature. The fun of catching and collecting "bugs" grew into an interest in observing living insects and other animals. They point out that there are great numbers of insects, most with short life spans, so killing a few for a collection has no impact on populations. However, certain butterflies, moths, and beetles should be left untouched (especially pollinators).

But now we have the best of both worlds. Like undercover FBI spies, we can use a small digital camera to make a virtual insect collection (think pixels, not pins). Capture a butterfly as it feeds on a flower. Upload it to the computer and zoom in on its mouth, its wings, its feet. Identify it and place it on a rap sheet with its relatives. Save it in an FBI most-wanted folder. Declassify it and share your suspect with the world.

Perhaps how we study insects—dead, alive, or virtual—depends on what we want to know. The important thing is to get outside, look closely, and discover the great big miniature world of insects in all its bugly wonder.

   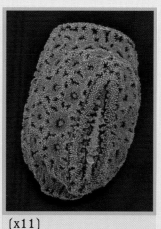 

(x9) (x11) (x8) (x11) (x9)

What is hidden in each of these exquisite microscopic insect containers? (Answer on p. 40)

GLOSSARY

Abdomen: The third section of an insect body located behind the head and thorax.

Antenna (plural: antennae): Feelerlike, segmented, flexible sense organ found in pairs on the head of an insect above its mouthparts or eyes.

Anther: The male part of the flower that produces and sheds pollen.

Bacteria: Microscopic single-celled organisms that feed off of plants, animals, and decaying matter; many species cause disease.

Biocontrol: Also called biological control, it is the means of controlling pests using predatory living organisms rather than lethal chemicals.

Bug: Insects with mouthparts that pierce and suck (Order Hemiptera). Often refers to any insect, spider, or disease-causing organism.

Bugly: Having insect qualities.

Caterpillar: The larval stage of a butterfly, moth, sawfly, or scorpionfly with a cylinder-shaped body, a head, and legs.

Chrysalis: A butterfly pupa.

Cocoon: A silken covering surrounding a pupa.

Coleoptera: The order of insects commonly called beetles that are characterized by chewing mouthparts and elytra (thickened forewings) that enclose membranous hind wings.

Compound eye: One of a pair of protruding eyes found on most adult insects and nymphs, consisting of a few to thousands of eye units (ommatidia).

Desperado: A criminal associated with the early settlement of the western United States.

Diptera: The order of insects commonly called true flies that have one pair of membranous wings and a pair of halters (knoblike appendages) instead of hind wings that help balance the insect during flight.

Elytra (singular: elytron): The thick, hard front wings of beetles that enclose the hind wings.

Exoskeleton: Hard outer covering of the arthropods (animals that include insects and their relatives, such as crustaceans and arachnids) that provides support and protection.

Facet: The outer surface, or lens, of each eye unit of a compound eye.

Family: A group of related organisms; family names end in –idae.

Felon: A criminal guilty of a serious crime.

Forager bee: Honeybees that leave the hive to search for food (pollen and nectar) and water.

Fruit: The part of a flowering plant that contains the seeds.

Fugitive: Someone who is running away or trying to escape.

Fungi: A group of plantlike organisms that do not contain chlorophyll (they are not green) and get their nutrients from dead or living organic matter.

Genera (singular: genus): Groups of closely related species. The genus is the first part of the two-part Latin scientific name of a species. The first letter is always capitalized, and the name is always underlined or italicized.

Grub: A thick larva with a head and legs.

Hemiptera: The insect order characterized by mouthparts that pierce and suck, commonly called true bugs. Most in this group have four wings with the front wings of many families having thickened bases and membranous tips ("half wings").

Hind wings: The pairs of wings on an insect located behind the forewings and attached to muscles in the thorax.

Hooligan: A young criminal.

Host: The plant or animal on which an organism, such as an insect, feeds.

Hymenoptera: The order of insects characterized by having four membranous wings with few veins.

Instar: The immature insect before it molts; most insects go through three to six instars.

Larva: The wormlike stage of an immature insect that emerges from the egg and develops into a pupa.

Lepidoptera: The order of insects characterized by having four wings with scales (butterflies and moths).

Maggot: A larva that lacks legs and a head.

Malaria: A deadly disease of the blood carried by several species of tropical mosquitoes.

Mandible: One of the two jaws that form the mouth of an insect.

Membranous: Consisting of a thin flexible sheet of living tissue that forms, covers, connects, or lines an organ.

Metamorphosis: The change in an insect's form during development.

Micrograph: A photograph of a specimen as seen through a microscope. An electron micrograph is the black-and-white image produced by an electron microscope.

Microscopic: Extremely small.

Molt: To shed the exoskeleton so the animal can grow.

Nematode: A round (cylinder-shaped) worm with a tough outer skin covering its unsegmented body.

Nocturnal: Refers to animals active only during the night.

Nymph: The immature stage of an insect that looks like a smaller copy of the adult (insects that undergo incomplete metamorphosis).

Odonata: The insect order that contains the dragonflies and damselflies; *odon* refers to the toothed jaws.

Ommatidium (plural: ommatidia): One of the many units that form the compound eye of an insect.

Order: A subdivision of a class (such as insects) of related organisms that is further divided into families.

Ovipositor: The external egg-laying structure found on many female insects.

Parasite: A living thing that lives and feeds on or inside the body of a host plant or animal.

Perception: The act of using the senses to gather information about the world.

Pest: An insect that damages plants, animals, and humans.

Pesticide: Poisonous chemicals that kill pests.

Pixel: An individual, tiny dot of light that is the basic unit of a digital image.

Pollen: Powdery material produced by flowering plants that contains the male reproductive cells.

Pollinate: The transfer of pollen grains from the male to the female that results in fertilization of the ovule (egg).

Pupa: The nonfeeding and usually inactive insect stage between the larva and the adult stages of complete metamorphosis.

Puparium: A hardened case that forms around a fly pupa.

Seed: The part of a plant found inside the fruit that contains the embryo that will grow into a new plant.

Segment: A small section or unit of the body, leg, or antenna found between flexible parts such as joints.

Setae: Hairs or bristles.

Species: Groups of populations found in nature that interbreed and produce young.

Stigma: The female part of a flower that receives male pollen grains.

Superorganism: A group of organisms, such as an insect colony, that work together and function as one social unit.

Tarsus (plural: tarsi): The last segment of an insect leg.

Thorax: The middle section of an insect body to which the legs and wings are attached.

True bugs: Insects with mouthparts that pierce and suck (Order Hemiptera).

Ultraviolet: Rays from the sun that are invisible to humans.

Virus: A tiny particle that can be an infectious agent in other living organisms, including humans.

SOURCES

BOOKS

Bland, Roger G., and H. E. Jaques. *How to Know the Insects.* 3rd ed. Dubuque, IA: Wm. C. Brown Company Publishers, 1978.

Borror, Donald J., and Richard E. White. *A Field Guide to the Insects of America North of Mexico.* Boston: Houghton Mifflin Company, 1970.

Dourlot, Sonia. *Insect Museum.* Ontario: Firefly Books, 2009.

Fabre, Jean-Henri. *The Insect World of J. Henri Fabre.* Translated by Alexander Teixeira Mattos. Boston: Beacon Press, 1991.

Goethe, Johann Wolfgang. *The Metamorphosis of Plants.* Cambridge: The MIT Press, 2009.

Hölldobler, Bert, and E. O. Wilson. *The Superorganism.* New York and London: W.W. Norton & Company, 2009.

Klots, Alexander B. *Butterflies of North America, East of the Great Plains.* Norwalk, CT: The Easton Press, 1951.

Klots, Elsie B. *The New Field Book of Freshwater Life.* New York: G. P. Putnam's Sons, 1966.

Raffles, Hugh. *Insectopedia.* New York: Pantheon Books, 2010.

Tilden, James W., and Arthur Clayton Smith. *Western Butterflies.* Norwalk, CT: The Easton Press, 1986.

Wilson, E. O. *Anthill.* New York and London: W.W. Norton & Company, 2010.

Yoon, Carol Kaesuk. *Naming Nature: The Clash Between Instinct and Science.* New York: W.W.Norton & Company, 2009.

ARTICLES

Grossman, Lisa. "Fruit Flies Maneuver on Autopilot." *Science News* (May 8, 2010): 8.

Saey, Tina Heman. "Foraging Bees Go with Their Guts. *Science News* (April 24, 2010): 16.

Stowasser, Annette, Alexandra Rapaport, John E. Layne, Randy C. Morgan, and Elke K. Buschbeck. "Biological Bifocal Lenses with Image Separation." *Current Biology,* 20, no.16 (24 August 2010): 1482–1486

Zimmer, Carl. "Blink Twice if You Like M." *The New York Times* (June 29, 2009).

MULTIMEDIA

Ants: Little Creatures Who Run the World. DVD. Boston: WGBH Educational Foundation, 1995, 2007.

Queen of the Sun: What are the Bees Telling Us? Directed by Tagart Siegel. Portland: Collective Eye, Inc., 2010.

http://courses.cit.cornell.edu/ ent201/content/eyes_lec.pdf

www.e-fabre.com/en/index.htm

http://gothamcitybees.com

http://insectopedia.org/heads.html

www.newyorker.com/fiction/ features/2010/01/25/100125fi_ fiction_wilson?currentPage=all

www.npr.org/templates/ story/story.php?storyId =125389428

www.nyc-bees.org

www.pollinator.org

www.scholarpedia.org/article/Insect_motion_ vision

www.talhalpern.org/archive

www.xerces.org

WEBSITES FOR STUDENTS AND TEACHERS

ASK A BIOLOGIST
http://askabiologist.asu.edu/home
This popular site sponsored by the Arizona State University holds an Ugly Bug Contest every year.

BUG SCOPE
http://bugscope.beckman.illinois.edu
The Bugscope project provides free interactive access to a scanning electron microscope (SEM) so that students anywhere in the world can explore the microscopic world of insects. This educational outreach program from the Beckman Institute's Imaging Technology Group at the University of Illinois supports K–16 classrooms worldwide.

DENNIS KUNKEL MICROSCOPY, INC.
http://education.denniskunkel.com/ MostWantedBugs.php
Dennis Kunkel has an educational website that has more of his photomicrographs as well as information about microscopy.

EARTH'S ENDANGERED CREATURES
www.earthsendangered.com/ search-groups-groups2sI.html
Earth's Endangered Creatures lists endangered plants and animals of the world that are threatened with extinction.

POLLINATOR PARTNERSHIP
www.pollinator.org
The Pollinator Partnership's mission is to protect pollinators, critical to food and ecosystems, through conservation, education, and research. Signature initiatives include the NAPPC (North American Pollinator Protection Campaign), National Pollinator Week, and the Ecoregional Planting Guides.

VIRTUAL MICROSCOPE
http://virtual.itg.uiuc.edu
The Virtual Microscope is a NASA-funded project that provides simulated scientific instrumentation for students and researchers worldwide as part of NASA's Virtual Laboratory initiative.

FIVE FASCINATING BOOKS ABOUT "BUGS"

Insect Museum (2009) by Sonia Dourlot is a lovely photographic work "describing 114 species of insects and other arthropods, including their natural history and environment." (Published in the United States by Firefly Books.)

Nic Bishop Butterflies and Moths (2009) by Nic Bishop is filled with amazing photographs and interesting facts. (Published by Scholastic Nonfiction.)

The Insect World of J. Henri Fabre is a collection of essays by the famed French entomologist (1823–1915) translated by Alexander Teixeira Mattos and reprinted in the 1991 edition by Beacon Press. E. O. Wilson commented: "The writings of Fabre are classic because they compose an accurate natural history of creatures all around us, written in a vivid personal style that will never grow old or tired."

The Hive Detectives: Chronicle of a Honey Bee Catastrophe (2010) by Loree Griffin Burns is a fascinating look at honeybees and the current threats they face. (Published by Houghton Mifflin Books for Children.)

Mosquito Bite (2005) by Alexandra Siy and Dennis Kunkel shows the life cycle of a mosquito in astonishing electron micrographs within the kid-friendly context of a summer evening's game of hide-and-seek. (Published by Charlesbridge.)

INDEX

Answer to p. 37: These are all egg cases that contain different species of walking sticks.